FIRST SCIENCE EXPERIMENTS

EXPERIMENTS WITH MATERIALS

By Anna Claybourne

WINDMILL BOOKS

Published in 2017 by **Windmill Books**, an Imprint of Rosen Publishing
29 East 21st Street, New York, NY 10010

Author: Anna Claybourne
Designer: Emma Randall
Illustrations: Caroline Romanet

CATALOGING-IN-PUBLICATION DATA

Names: Claybourne, Anna. Title: Experiments with materials / Anna Claybourne.
Description: New York : Windmill Books, 2017. | Series: First science experiments | Includes index.
Identifiers: ISBN 9781508192442 (pbk.) | ISBN 9781508192404 (library bound) | ISBN 9781508192329 (6 pack)
Subjects: LCSH: Matter--Properties--Experiments--Juvenile literature.
Classification: LCC QC173.36 C627 2017 | DDC 530.4078--dc23

Manufactured in the United States of America
CPSIA Compliance Information: Batch #BS16PK: For Further Information contact Rosen Publishing, New York, New York at 1-800-237-9932

Contents

Introduction

Science means finding out about the world, and all the stuff in it. That's why scientists do experiments – to find out as much as they can!

Science tips

- Clear a neat, empty space for doing experiments in.
- Check if it's OK to use the things in the "You will need" boxes with whoever owns them!
- For messy experiments, wear old clothes, not your best outfit!
- Do messy experiments outdoors, if you can.
- Remember to clean up the mess afterwards!

GET AN ADULT ASSISTANT

For some of the experiments, you'll need to heat things, cook things, chop things up, or use electrical items. For anything like this, make sure you have an adult handy to help you.

KEEPING RECORDS

Real scientists don't just do experiments - they also keep records. To do this, you could take photos of your experiments or draw pictures of them, and write down what happened.

Try it yourself!

This book is full of easy but exciting experiments for you to try for yourself. For most of them, you only need a few basic things that you can find at home.

Are you ready to experiment? Turn the page and let's get started!

Materials

Reach out your hand and touch something. Wherever you are, whatever you're doing, you'll be surrounded by real, 3-D stuff that you can feel. There are many different types of this stuff, and they are known as "materials."

Useful materials

We need materials for making things. Without them, we wouldn't have homes, clothes, books, computers or anything else. But when we use materials, we have to pick the right one for the job. The properties of each material decide what it can be used for.

Socks are made out of strong, soft fibers, like cotton or wool.

What would be a really bad thing to make socks out of?

Try this!

Find a pen and paper, and set a timer for 2 minutes. In that time, how many different materials can you find in your home or classroom (or wherever you happen to be)? Write them down.

TYPES OF MATERIALS

All the things around us, even our own bodies, are made of materials. There are thousands of types of materials. Here are just a few of them.

Some materials are found in nature, and are easy to find.

Water

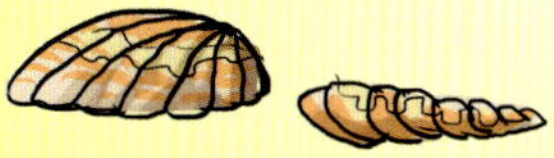

Shells

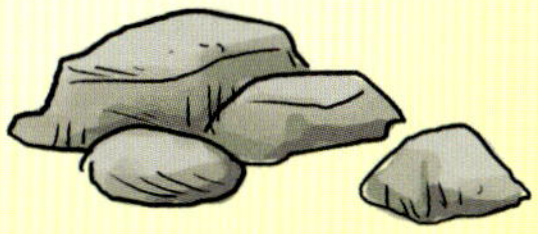

Rocks

Wood

Some materials come from nature, but we have to get them out, or extract them.

Iron (comes from some types of rocks)

Sunflower oil (from sunflower seeds)

Cotton (from the cotton plant)

Some materials are made by humans, using the natural materials we find around us.

Paper

Plastic

Paint

Concrete

PROPERTIES

Each material has its own properties - how it behaves and what it can do. For example, bamboo is strong and light. Rubber is stretchy and tough.

Testing, testing!

To find out what a material's properties are, scientists have to do tests. How strong is it? How stretchy is it? Is it waterproof? Is it see-through? Try testing some materials yourself!

You will need:

- A selection of small everyday objects. Here are some ideas, but you could use other things too.
  - Coin
  - Wooden matchstick
  - Seashell
  - Cork
  - Metal paper clip
  - Plastic button
  - Eraser
  - Small piece of paper
  - Plastic sandwich bag
  - Small carrot
  - Sponge
  - Rubber band
  - Pebble
  - Modeling clay
  - Square of chocolate
  - Sock
- A large bowl or bucket full of water
- A magnet

TEST 1: DOES IT FLOAT?

Try putting each object into the bowl or bucket of water, to see if it floats or not.

Tip!
These objects will endure some tough testing. So try not to use anything precious that you're not allowed to break!

In the charts

Real scientists write down what happens in their experiments. You could make a chart for each test to show your results.

Object	Floats	Does not float!
Coin		√
Matchstick	√	
Seashell		√
Cork	√	

TEST 2: BEND OR BREAK?

Can you tear, break or rip the object with your hands?

Try this!

Can you think of any other tests you could try?

TEST 3: THE MAGNET TEST

See if your magnet pulls the object towards it.

What has happened?

Each material has its own properties, depending on what it is made of, and how it is made. For example, a thin piece of wood is easy to snap, while a coin isn't. Cork floats easily, while a seashell will sink. What would each material be good for making?

Melted crayon art

Materials can change as they heat up and cool down. This is called "changing state." Try this experiment to see how crayons melt and harden again – and make some art too!

1 Tape several crayons along the top of the card stock, pointing downward. Lean it up against a wall or chair, with newspaper underneath to catch any drips.

You will need:

- Old crayons
- A hair dryer (and an adult to help)
- Strong sticky tape
- A thick, stiff piece of card stock (white if possible)
- Newspaper

Try this!
If you don't have a hair dryer, it may work to leave the card stock in hot sunshine.

2 Switch on the hair dryer and blow hot air at the crayons for a minute or two.

3 As the crayons start to melt and drip, tip the card stock to help the runny wax make patterns. Let the picture cool.

What has happened?

As the crayons melt, they change from a solid into a liquid, and run down. When they cool the wax turns solid again.

The shrinking puddle

Materials can also change from a liquid into a gas. Gases are very spread out, and can disappear into the air. Watch this happen with a puddle!

You will need:

- Some water
- A bowl
- An outdoor space
- A dry, warm, sunny day
- Chalk

1 Take some water in a bowl and pour a bit onto the ground to make a puddle.

2 Draw around the puddle with the chalk.

3 Keep checking the puddle every half hour or so, and draw around it.

What has happened?

As the sun and ground heat the water, it slowly turns into a gas, or "evaporates." The gas, called water vapor, escapes into the air. The puddle shrinks from the edges, because more heat can reach there from the surrounding ground.

Ice tower

Many materials freeze, or set hard, as they get cooler – like the wax crayons. Normally, when they are frozen, they take up less space. But when water freezes, it gets bigger!

You will need:

- A small plastic water bottle (open)
- Water
- A freezer

1 Fill the bottle right up to the top with water.

Another fun idea

What happens if you freeze a bottle of water, and a bottle of sunflower oil, both full to the brim?

2 Put it in the freezer (make sure there is a bit of space above it).

3 Leave it to freeze overnight, then take it out.

What has happened?

As the water freezes, it grows slightly. It has nowhere to go but out of the top of the bottle. It pushes up and forms a “tower” of ice.

Melt ice with salt

You will need:

- A few plastic bowls
- Water
- Salt
- A freezer
- Large trays or shallow plastic boxes
- Watercolor paints or food coloring
- Teaspoons

Water usually freezes into ice below 32° F (0° C). Above that temperature, it melts again. But you can melt ice another way, using salt.

1

Fill the bowls with water and freeze them overnight to make blocks of ice.

2

Turn each ice block out into a tray. Then sprinkle them with some salt.

3

Look closely. Can you see the ice turning into water?

Using a spoon, drip runny watercolor paint or food coloring onto the ice to reveal what the water is doing.

What has happened?

Salty water freezes at a lower temperature than normal water. That's one reason the sea doesn't freeze very easily! When you add salt to ice, it helps it to melt. The colors show you where the water is flowing.

The exploding bag

When some materials mix together, it leads to a "chemical reaction." As the materials combine, they change, and make something new. In this experiment, you can make gas fill a bag until it pops!

1 Put about six teaspoons of baking soda onto a piece of toilet paper. Fold up the paper around it to make a little package.

You will need:

- A plastic sandwich bag with an airtight seal
- Vinegar
- Baking soda (from the baking section in a supermarket)
- Hot tap water
- Cup
- Teaspoon
- Toilet paper
- An outdoor area

2 Outdoors, hold the bag upright and put in about half a cupful of vinegar, and quarter of a cupful of hot water.

Another fun idea

What happens if you mix the ingredients in a cup? (Make sure you do this outside too, or over a sink!)

3

Put the paper package inside the top of the bag, and hold it there while you seal up the opening tightly.

4

Then let the package drop into the vinegar. The vinegar and the baking soda will begin to react.

5

Can you see bubbles of gas forming? How long does it take for the gas to fill up the bag? Don't stand too close - if you're lucky, it will pop!

What has happened?

The baking soda and the vinegar contain different types of materials, or chemicals. They react together to make a type of gas, carbon dioxide. The gas spreads out to fill up the bag, and pushes against it from the inside.

Turn coins green

Coins like pennies contain the metal copper. It's normally a pinkish-brown color, but after being used a lot, these coins turn darker and dirtier. Let's turn them green instead!

1 Half-fill the cup with white vinegar and add a teaspoon of salt. Stir until it disappears.

You will need:

- Several copper coins (the brownish-colored ones)
- White vinegar
- Salt
- A cup
- A teaspoon
- A shallow bowl
- Paper towels

2 Put a paper towel into the bottom of the bowl and arrange the coins on top.

3 Sprinkle vinegar over the coins so that they all get wet, but are not totally covered.

4

Take a few of the coins out and wash them in water, then leave them to dry on another paper towel.

Another fun idea

Look out for bright green roofs and statues when you're out and about. They are made of copper that has reacted with the air.

5

Leave the rest of the coins in the vinegar. Add a bit more vinegar if it dries out.

6

After a few hours, compare the two groups of coins. Do they look different?

What has happened?

The salt and vinegar mixture cleans the coins, making them bright and shiny. But those that stay in the vinegar start to turn green! This is because the vinegar helps the copper to react with a gas, oxygen, in the air. This makes a new, green material called copper oxide.

Invisible ink

Write an invisible secret message that can't be seen... then use chemical reactions to make it appear! What will your message say?

1

Pour or squeeze your lemon juice into the bowl. Spread out your paper flat to write on.

You will need:

- Paper
- Lemon juice
- A small bowl
- A paintbrush or cotton swab
- A warm radiator or a hair dryer

2

Dip your paintbrush or cotton swab in the juice and use it to write your secret message on the paper. (It will be easier if your message is quite short.)

Try this!

Send a secret message through the mail to a friend or relative, and ask them to send you one back!

3 Leave your paper somewhere cool and flat to dry. Once it's dry, you can give or send it to someone.

Another fun idea

Some other materials can also work as invisible ink. Try apple juice, lemonade or white vinegar, and see if they work as well.

4 To see the message, the other person needs to heat up the paper. They can leave it on a hot radiator for a while, or heat it with a hair dryer. Ta-daa! - the message is revealed!

What has happened?

Many materials, such as lemon juice, react when they are heated. This makes them change, and sometimes change color. The juice turns brown as it gets hotter. You can also see this happening when you cook some types of food, such as toast, cake and onions.

Make your own butter

Some materials are mixtures. They contain two or more different things mixed together. Milk and cream are like this. You can't see it, but they are made of tiny bits of fat mixed into a watery liquid. How can you get them apart?

You will need:

- Some heavy or whipping cream
- A jar or plastic container with a tight-fitting lid
- Strong arms!
- Cold water
- A bowl or butter dish

1 If possible, leave the cream out of the fridge for a while first. It works best at room temperature.

2 Make sure your container or jar is clean and dry. Pour in your cream and put the lid on tightly.

3 Start shaking! Hold the container or jar firmly and shake it up and down, up and down.

4 It takes a lot of shaking, so you might need to swap arms, or take turns with friends or family.

5 Eventually, you will feel the cream get thicker, then start to make a slapping sound. You'll see it has separated into a lump of butter and a runny, watery liquid called buttermilk.

6 Take the butter out, carefully rinse it in cold water, and put it in a dish. Try it spread on toast!

Another fun idea

If you save the buttermilk that's left behind, you can use it to make pancakes or soda bread. Look on the Web or in a cookbook for a recipe.

What has happened?

As you shake the cream, the tiny bits of fat inside it keep banging into each other. Every time they do, they stick together, making bigger and bigger lumps. Finally, they all clump into one lump, separated from the watery liquid (the buttermilk).

Make salt crystals

When you stir salt or sugar into water, it disappears! But it hasn't really gone anywhere. It has dissolved – broken down into tiny bits that are mixed into the water. Some materials can dissolve, and then form again as shapes called crystals.

You will need:

- Salt
- Hot water
- A small, heatproof measuring jug
- A teaspoon
- String
- A pencil

1

With an adult to help, half-fill the jug with very hot tap water or almost-boiling water. Stir in 10 teaspoons of salt.

2

Keep stirring until the salt disappears. Keep adding more salt and stirring, until there is a bit of salt left at the bottom that won't dissolve.

3 Tie a short piece of string to the middle of the pencil. Balance the pencil over the jug so that the string dangles down into the water.

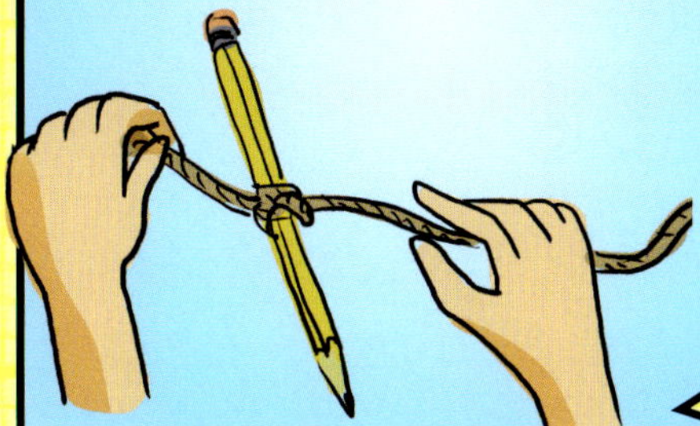

4 Now leave the jug in a safe place for a few days, and check it every day. You should see the crystals starting to grow on the string.

Another fun idea

Try adding a bit of food coloring to the water. Can you make colored crystals?

5 When the string is covered in crystals, you can take it out and look at them closely. Can you see what shape they are?

Try this!

You could look at your crystals even more closely, using a magnifying glass or microscope.

What has happened?

The salt dissolves in the hot water and breaks down into tiny bits. But as the water cools, the bits start to clump together again. Gradually, the water evaporates (turns into a gas), leaving the salt behind. The string gives the crystals a good place to stick to, so they start forming there.

Oobleck!

Water, milk and oil are liquids. Rock, plastic and wood are solids. But oobleck is a bit different! It can behave like a solid or a liquid, depending on what you do with it.

You will need:

- Cornstarch
- Water
- A plastic container
- A measuring cup
- A spoon
- Lots of newspaper to catch the drips!

1 Fill the measuring cup to the brim with water and pour it into the container. Fill the cup with cornstarch and carefully add the cornstarch to the water. Stir it in.

2 Fill the cup with cornstarch again, and stir in more and more cornstarch until you have a thick, gloppy mixture (you may need almost all of the second cup).

Try this!
Color your oobleck by adding a few drops of food coloring to the water at the start.

3 Now put the container on some newspaper, and try playing with the oobleck. What happens if you stir it slowly? What happens if you try to stir it as fast as you can?

4 Try to grab a handful of oobleck and squeeze it hard to form a ball. What happens when you let go?

5 Sink your hand into the oobleck, then try to pull it out suddenly. What if you pull it out slowly? You could try the same experiment with a toy plastic figure too.

Tip:
When you've finished, the oobleck can be washed away with warm water.

What has happened?

Oobleck is a strange material. When it's pressed hard, the grains of cornstarch lock together, and it can seem solid. When it's handled slowly, it flows and runs like a liquid. There are materials like this in nature too, such as quicksand.

Materials for building

We use materials to build all kinds of things – houses, shops, schools, bridges, towers and tunnels. And we have to be sure they won't fall to pieces! Experiment with different materials and methods to see how strong you can make your structures.

You will need:

- Dry spaghetti
- Marshmallows
- Wooden popsicle sticks
- Loom bands or small elastic bands
- Tape measure

1 First, try building towers using just spaghetti and marshmallows. Use the marshmallows to hold the ends of the spaghetti sticks together.

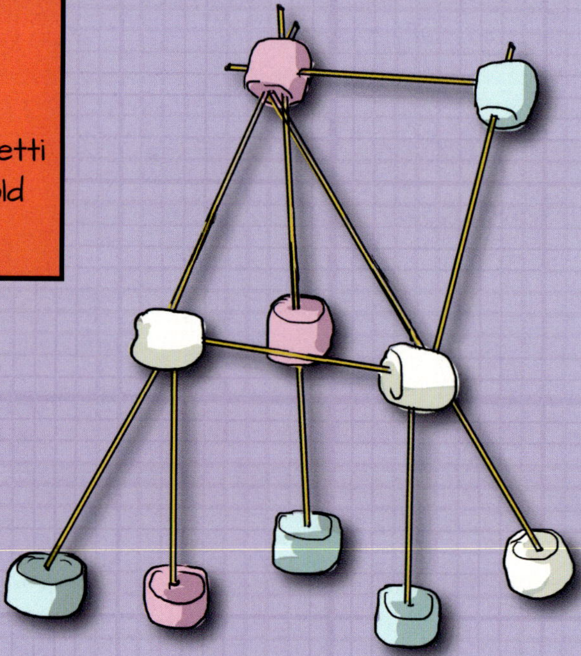

2 What shapes can you make? How can you use these materials to make a tower? How can you make it stronger?

3 Now try building using popsicle sticks and stretchy elastic bands. Wrap the bands around the ends of the sticks to hold them together in different positions.

4 How can you make your popsicle stick buildings as tall as possible? Do you need to use different building methods and designs?

5 The spaghetti and marshmallows are not very strong, but they are very light. The popsicle sticks and elastic bands are stronger, but also much heavier. Which do you think is best for building?

Another fun idea

With friends or family, form two teams, one using spaghetti and one using popsicle sticks. Who can build the tallest tower?

What has happened?

Just like real architects and builders, you have to work out how to use your materials to get the most out of their properties – the things they can do.

Thinking about... materials

When water freezes, the ice always floats on top. That's because as it freezes it gets bigger and takes up more space - so ice is lighter than water. Floating ice makes ice floes and icebergs.

Why do we hang laundry out? Because the water in it will evaporate, especially in the warm sunshine. Result: nice dry clothes!

Old iron objects get rusty because of a chemical reaction between materials. Iron reacts with water and oxygen gas in the air. This makes crumbly, reddish-brown iron oxide, or rust.
Bridges have to be very strong, to carry traffic and survive high winds. But they also have to be light enough to stay up! They often use steel, formed into strong, light cables - like this suspension bridge in South Carolina.

Further information

Books

Amazing Science: Materials by Sally Hewitt (Wayland, 2014)

Experiments in Material and Matter with Toys and Everyday Stuff by Natalie Rompella (Capstone Press, 2015)

Mind Webs: Materials by Anna Claybourne (Wayland, 2014)

Ways into Science: Everyday Materials by Peter Riley (Franklin Watts, 2014)

Websites

For web resources related to the subject of this book, go to: **www.windmillbooks.com/weblinks** and select this book's title.

Glossary

chemical reaction
A process where substances undergo a change to form a different substance

chemicals
Substances produced by or used in a process of change (chemical reaction).

crystal
A solid material that forms itself into a repeating 3-D pattern.

dissolve
To mix with a liquid and become part of the liquid.

evaporates
Turns from a liquid into a gas.

fibers
Fine threads of material that can be spun to make wool or made into cloth.

float
To rest on the surface of a liquid, without sinking.

freeze
To cool something to a very low temperature, usually forming ice.

gas
A substance that is like air and has no fixed shape.

magnet
An object that is able to pull some types of metal towards it.

properties
Describes what a material is like and how it behaves.

water vapor
Water that has evaporated and is in the form of gas.

waterproof
Does not allow water to pass through.

Index